·ᖚ fuel ᒐ presents

INUA ELLAMS'
BLACK
T-SHIRT
COLLECTION

Written and performed by **Inua Ellams**
Directed by **Thierry Lawson**
Designed by **Michael Vale**
Lighting Design by **Michael Nabarro**
Sound Design by **Emma Laxton**
Graphic Design by **Inua Ellams**

Commissioned by Warwick Arts Centre. Developed with
the support of the Arvon Foundation and the National
Theatre. Funded by Arts Council England.

LOTTERY FUNDED

Inua Ellams

Inua Ellams is a poet, playwright and performer. He has lived in Jos, Plateau State – Nigeria, Dublin – Ireland and London – England, where he currently resides. He has five books published, including his most recent pamphlet of poems *Candy Coated Unicorns and Converse All Stars* (Flipped Eye, 2011).

He also works as a graphic designer/visual artist, as such describes himself as a 'Word & Graphic Artist'. As a workshop facilitator, he has taught in universities, secondary schools, primary schools, theatres, libraries and museums, delivering prose, poetry, occasionally combined with visual art as a stimulus in cross art form workshops. He also delivers workshops through social media networks such as Twitter & Facebook.

His first play *The 14th Tale,* won a Fringe First Award at the Edinburgh Festival Fringe 2009 before touring nationally and transferring to the National Theatre in spring 2010. He will be performing the play for its international debut at Perth Festival 2012 in February. His second play, *Untitled*, was long listed for the Alfred Fagon award. It was co-commissioned by Soho Theatre and toured nationally in autumn 2010.

Thierry Lawson

Thierry Lawson likes to brand himself as a storyteller whether as a theatre director, a workshop leader, a film-maker or when venturing into the realm of performing. His work has taken him to many various and challenging horizons, gathering accolades, awards and friends, often ignoring the advice 'don't diversify too much'. From proscenium arches to prisons, disused warehouses to film studios, national theatres to estates, somewhere someone has a story that relates to us and needs to be told.

His work has been nominated and won various awards to date. Thierry is Associate Director for Arc Theatre and Tam Tam Theatre cy.

Forever 'l'artiste sans frontieres'.

Michael Vale

Michael has designed the sets and costumes for over 170 theatre and opera productions both in the UK and abroad including those he has directed.

Companies he has worked with include: the Royal Shakespeare Company; the National Theatre; the Royal Opera House, Covent Garden; English National Opera; Glyndebourne Festival Opera; Opera North; English Touring Opera: De Vlaamse Opera, Antwerp; Los Angeles Opera; New Zealand International Art's Festival; Galaxy Theatre, Tokyo; Warsaw Globe Theatre Company; Munich Biennalle: Lyric Hammersmith; Almeida Theatre; Manchester Royal Exchange; West Yorkshire Playhouse; Sheffield Crucible; Northampton Theatre Royal; Liverpool Playhouse; Nottingham Playhouse; Bristol Old Vic; Plymouth Theatre Royal; Edinburgh Royal Lyceum; Bolton Octagon; Oldham Coliseum; Manchester Library Theatre; Salisbury Playhouse; Colchester Mercury Theatre; English Touring Theatre; the Royal Festival Hall; the Queen Elizabeth Hall; The Sage, Gateshead; BAC; Told By An Idiot, Spymonkey and Kneehigh Theatre Company.

His work has been nominated for two Olivier Awards; a Charrington Fringe First Award; an Irish Times Theatre Award and a Manchester Evening News Theatre Award.

Michael Nabarro

Michael's recent lighting designs include *The 14th Tale* (Cottesloe Theatre & touring); *Untitled* (Bristol Old Vic, Soho Theatre & touring); *Shalom Baby* (Theatre Royal Stratford East); *The World's Wife* (Trafalgar Studios & touring); *Ghosts in the Gallery* (Polka Theatre); *Coming Home*, *The Ballad of Crazy Paola*, *The Lady from the Sea*, *An Enemy of the People* & *The Blind* (Arcola Theatre); *Our Share of Tomorrow*, *Lough/Rain*, *Limbo* & *1984* (York Theatre Royal); *Slaves*, *Beasts* & *Cocoa* (Theatre503).

Michael is a graduate of the RADA Lighting Design course. He previously graduated from Cambridge University and spent three years managing the ADC Theatre in Cambridge. Michael is also the Managing Director of Spektrix, a provider of cloud-based ticketing systems to the Arts industry.

Emma Laxton

Current and forthcoming productions include: *Making Noise Quietly* and *The Physicists* (Donmar Warehouse); *Lay Down Your Cross* and *Blue Heart Afternoon* (Hampstead Theatre); *Lady Windermere's Fan* (Royal Exchange).

Emma's recent Sound Designs include: *The Recruiting Officer* (Donmar Warehouse); *Invisible* (Transport UK Tour & Luxembourg); *One Monkey Don't Stop No Show* (Sheffield Theatres/Eclipse UK Tour); *Much Ado About Nothing* (Wyndhams Theatre, West End); *Precious Little Talent* (Trafalgar Studios); *Charged* (Clean Break, Soho Theatre); *Men Should Weep* (National Theatre); *My Romantic History* (Sheffield Theatres and Bush Theatre); *Sisters*, *The Unthinkable* (Sheffield Theatres); *Pornography* (Birmingham Rep/Traverse and Tricycle Theatre).

Emma was previously Deputy Head of Sound for the Royal Court where she designed numerous productions including: *The Westbridge* (& Theatre Local), *The Heretic*, *Off The Endz!*, *Tusk Tusk*, *That Face* (and Duke of York's Theatre, West End), *Gone Too Far!*, *My Name Is Rachel Corrie* (and Playhouse Theatre, West End, Minetta Lane Theatre, New York, Galway Festival and Edinburgh Festival).

Emma is the Associate Sound Designer for the National Theatre's production of *War Horse* and was previously an Associate Artist at the Bush Theatre.

·fueL

Black T-shirt Collection is produced by **Fuel**. Fuel produces fresh work for adventurous people by inspiring artists. Founded in 2004 and led by Louise Blackwell and Kate McGrath, Fuel is a producing organisation working in partnership with some of the most exciting theatre artists in the UK to develop, create and present new work for all.

Fuel is currently producing projects with Will Adamsdale, Belarus Free Theatre, Clod Ensemble, Inua Ellams, Fevered Sleep, David Rosenberg, Sound&Fury, Uninvited Guests and Melanie Wilson. In partnership with higher education organisations, Fuel runs a rolling internship scheme. For further information on Fuel, our artists, our team and our internships, please visit www.fueltheatre.com or call 020 7228 6688.

Fuel's recent projects include: *The Simple Things in Life* (various artists); *Minsk 2011: A Reply to Kathy Acker* (Belarus Free Theatre); *Jackson's Way* (Will Adamsdale); *Electric Hotel* (Requardt & Rosenberg); *Kursk* and *Going Dark* Sound&Fury); *MUST: The Inside Story* (Peggy Shaw and Clod Ensemble); *Love Letters Straight From Your Heart* (Uninvited Guests); *The Forest* and *On Ageing* (Fevered Sleep); *The 14th Tale* (Inua Ellams); *An Anatomie in Four Quarters* (Clod Ensemble) and *Autobiographer* (Melanie Wilson).

"One of the most exciting and indispensable producing outfits working in British theatre today."
Guardian

"The maverick producing organisation who are prepared to invest in adventurous artists."
The Herald

Directors **Louise Blackwell** & **Kate McGrath**
Executive Director **Ed Errington**
Producer **Christina Elliot**
Head of Production **Stuart Heyes**
Project Managers **Alice Massey** & **Rosalind Wynn**
Deputy Production Manager **Ian Moore**
Administrator **Natalie Dibsdale**

Make Your Mark on Fuel:

At Fuel we are constantly working with artists to create new experiences for you to enjoy. We believe in these aims and work hard every day to make them happen. If you would like to make your mark, visit our website at fueltheatre.com and click on 'support'. There are lots of ways you can get involved. Just £5 a month will help make our ambitions real. In return we'll give you exclusive benefits and the inside story on what we're up to. You'll make great ideas come to life for the broadest possible audience.

You'll keep us going.

To get involved, please download the Make Your Mark form from the Fuel website: www.fueltheatre.com

Thank you from all of us.

A big thank you to our current supporters:

   JERWOOD CHARITABLE FOUNDATION

Fuel receives National Portfolio funding from Arts Council England.

With thanks to our catalysts:
Sean Egan, James Mackenzie-Blackman, Michael Morris, Sarah Preece, Sarah Quelch, John Tiffany and Nick Williams.

Tour dates

Unity Theatre, Liverpool
9–10 March
unitytheatreliverpool.co.uk

Rose Theatre
Edge Hill University Ormskirk
12 March
edgehill.ac.uk/rosetheatre

Contact, Manchester
13–14 March
contactmcr.com

Bristol Old Vic
15–17 March
bristololdvic.org.uk

Hawth Studio, Crawley
26–27 March
hawth.co.uk

National Theatre, London
12–24 April
nationaltheatre.org.uk

Parabola Arts Centre, Cheltenham
27 April
parabolaartscentre.co.uk

Warwick Arts Centre, Coventry
1–2 May
warwickartscentre.co.uk

The Maltings Theatre, Berwick-upon-Tweed
5 May
maltingsberwick.co.uk

The Basement
as part of caravan at Brighton Festival
13 May
brightonfestival.org

Merlin Theatre, Frome
14 May
merlintheatre.co.uk

BLACK T-SHIRT COLLECTION

INUA ELLAMS'
BLACK
T-SHIRT
COLLECTION

OBERON BOOKS
LONDON

WWW.OBERONBOOKS.COM

First published in 2012 by Oberon Books Ltd
521 Caledonian Road, London N7 9RH
Tel: +44 (0) 20 7607 3637 / Fax: +44 (0) 20 7607 3629
e-mail: info@oberonbooks.com
www.oberonbooks.com

Reprinted in 2012

A catalogue record for this book is available from the British
Library.

PB ISBN: 978-1-84943-191-0
E ISBN: 978-1-84943-295-5

Cover image by Franklyn Rodgers
www.franklynrodgers.com

Printed and bound by CPI Group (UK) Ltd, Croydon, CR0 4YY.

Visit www.oberonbooks.com to read more about all our books
and to buy them. You will also find features, author interviews and
news of any author events, and you can sign up for e-newsletters
so that you're always first to hear about our new releases.

In chronological order, thanks to:

James T. Kirk, Jean-Luc Picard, Benjamin Sisko, Kathryn Janeway, Krystle Lai, Kate McGrath, Louise Blackwell, Christina Elliot, NPR's Planet Money Podcast Team: Jacob Goldstein, Alex Bloomberg, Adam Davidson, Hannah Jaffe Walsh, Thierry Lawson, Ed Collier, Paul Warwick, Alan Ryvet, Nii Parkes, Nina Steiger, Kayo Chingonyi, Ore Disu, Samuel Sabo, Felicia Okoye, Danella Officer, Nadia Latif, Sabrina Mafhous, Simon Block, Frances Poet, Shiui Weng, Nick Starr, Sebastian 'Bash' Born, Gabbi Wong, Dipo Salimonu, James Baldwin, Roz Wynn, Ed Errington & the other angel-feathered folk at Fuel, Vicki Heathcock, Michael Vale, Michael Nabarro, Michael Alebiosu, Danielle Evans, Connie Abbe, Gabrielle Smith, Franklyn Rodgers, Charlotte Wilkinson, Lupe Fiasco, Estabrak Al-Ansari, Shehab El-Tawil, Martin Roberts and the ever relentless Ellams.

Dedicated to the bridge-builders of our time
& to Josh & Musa. (Just talk. Please.)

FRAGMENTS OF BONE

Let me begin again, I say, as the bar blurs
invisible, its volume reduced to the merest
suggestion of others and it's just us spotlit
in the black womb-like silence of theatre
and your question themes the play; let me
begin again: I went to church last Sunday.

The pastor preached: put not your faith in
man who only is good as his next breath;
align your faith with he who gives breath.
Here I stutter, my answer splintering like
fragments of bone against the mud soil
of memory. Moments before, I recalled

the call to prayer: In the Name of Allah
Most Gracious, Most Merciful – the slow
unfurling Imam's son's voice as dusk
touched the courtyard, the dust settling,
the sun solemnly bowed on the horizon –
thin as a prayer mat – and the gathered
performing ablutions: Bismillah, they say,
washing hands, mouths, nostrils, faces,
arms, head, ears, feet, kneeling to pray
Allah Is Great, God Is Great, they say.

You counter with airplanes, fireballs,
towers falling; stop your rant with
the first fireman to die, his skull caved
by a jumper from the 51st floor fleeing
flames. In the name of Allah, Gracious,
Great, Merciful this was done, you say.

I mention Amazing Grace, how sweet
the choir leader swayed in white robes,
eyes closed, humming southern baptist
hymn hypnotic, sailing congregations
to the oceanic depth whence his tears:
wide and sure as waves ride back and
forth that everything would be all right.

You rejected faith again, describing Jos,
Nigeria, the girl watching flat amongst
tall grass: the squad of Christian men
who hold her mother down as another
swings down with a machete, down as
sunlight skates the blade's edge, down,
the last swing, the fragments of bone
and there are screams no more.

There's blood in the drama of Men and
Gods, you say: rivers of it flow through
our wounded earth, gush from scripts
in houses of worship and act after act
aren't all stained? except the audience?
the secular astray? You gesture toward
those seated in darkness who gawk as we
squabble on stage; Aren't they the ones
the light beyond will touch unbloodied?
who will die hands clean?

… Let me begin again, I say, I went to
church/the pastor preached/faith/man
/breath/… I stutter, the bar blurs back
to life, words fall against your ears.

'For, while the tale of how we suffer, and how we are delighted, and how we may triumph is never new, it always must be heard. There isn't any other tale to tell, it's the only light we've got in all this darkness.'
James Baldwin, *Sonny's Blues*

PART 1 //

Sound –

A man moving around in darkness.

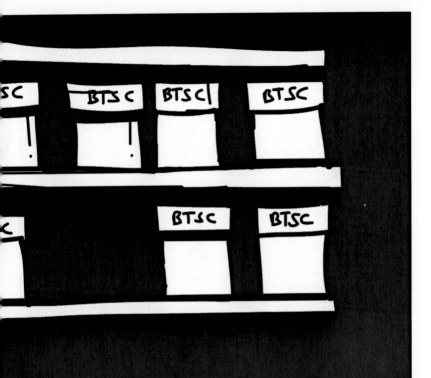

Matthew is struck dumb by the brightness on the landing; he squints, his eyes like tadpoles scurry from the light, he tries to hide behind the box as if he were small enough **– Welcome –** Ayah, the sister says **– We knew you'd come, come to the parlour, I've been waiting, so has Mum –**

He trembles in the living room's stifling darkness and nothing's changed since the wake, weeks ago. Night squeezes through slits in the curtain, she says nothing but Halima, the mother, she is sat on the left. At the far end, a floor lamp is lit. Its low glow licks the rich thick carpet and flowers drooping in the humid heat. Ayah, the sister, takes her chair and begins:

– So, I heard you punched the pastor on Sunday? He's fine, think you fractured his jaw, but you've done it this time, some cracks don't heal? Why'd you do that to him? Eh? Matthew, They say you want to close the shop? It's all you've got since… –

Her tongue fails her, mouth suddenly dry and Matthew finishes **– since Muhammed died? –** Ayah curls up, knees to her chest. There's nothing save her muffled sobbing, just breath and darkness. Across the room her mother, Halima, who'd spoken not a word, lifts her head lightly like a morning mist, lifts, dignified, the way queens do, whispers **– Tell me how he died. Tell me how he died. TELL ME HOW MY SON DIED, YOU BASTARD BOY, YOU WILL KILL ME IN THIS HOUSE! YOU WILL KILL ME O! Tell me how my son –**

– He loved you – Ayah says as Halima, her mother cries **– You were his favourite story to tell, he'd stop board meetings, bank managers, bar tenders, lean over, order that stupid drink of Scottish Scotch and Ribena, lean forward and say 'It all started with him you know' –** Muhammed would say 'Way back when we were boys, I ran with some bastard guys eh! Naija's answer to John Travolta! Greased back hair, tight black jeans, trying to enter clubs or smoking, watching girls. All the small boys wanted to be like us you know, so we'd send them on impossible tasks "Sssss! Aeyssss! Small boy, come here. Take this 5 Naira, go to the shop, buy me 2 fried fish, 3 bottles of coke, 1 Fanta, 6 packs of cabin biscuits, 3 Guinness, 2 Moimoi, 7 Tomtoms and 9, no 10, 11…20 chewing sticks. Oya GO! Ayessss! I want my change O!" Impossible! Anyway, it was Matthew's turn and Zebra Santana, that was his nickname, don't ask, Zebra Santana sent him. But Matthew did what we hated most, returned empty handed, sniffing, crying as if all the desert dust had blown into his eyes. Zebra Santana just runs, kicks him in his chest, Matthew lands and bounces in the sand, doesn't move. I go, punch Santana to the ground, then "Matthew, bro you OK?" And Matthew, he unfurls, slow, like a dust flower, except, he is looking at his black shirt. Santana's footprint: stamped on his chest; perfect stone crystals glinting in the grooves. Bro looks at me with his little, big eyes, says "Let's go home" I lift him and he says to mum 'D'you have some black cloth?' and copied the footprint pattern from the shirt. Next day we set up shop. Zebra Santana was the first customer after he apologised. We sold 30 shirts in 2 days and that was it! Black T-shirt Collection, thank you, Bob's your uncle, gimme the cash, over and out! All started with him you know!' **– He loved you –** Ayah says **– Now you want to dismantle his life's work? –**

So this is about Muhammed. Musaddiq Zango, walking home from work, was stopped by a group of Christian men, vexed at a beheading of their brethren in the city of Kano, north of where they stood. They asked Musaddiq what he thought of this. He replied it wasn't his business and tried to walk away. Muhammed was twelve, Ayah was five when their father, Musaddiq, Halima's husband died. Halima banned religion from her house. One month passed and Halima returns with Matthew from a children's home **– Kids, this is your brother –** They wished to fill the void Musaddiq left with someone to look after, one who needed love. This was unheard of at the time, a

Christian boy fostered in a Muslim house. Matthew was just seven, he clenched the hem of Halima's wrapper, a slow breeze twirled a loose dangling thread, he snapped it off. Muhammed smiled **– Would you like to be my friend? –** his arm stretched out like an olive branch.

They grew tight after that, inseparable friends of scuffed knees and stone-throwing-sand-magic, salt of the earth type of childhood living in Jos, Plateau State, Nigeria. When violence broke out between Muslims and Christians with casualties reported on both sides, Halima tried to hide the kids from it. Still some days, Muhammed returned with bruised fists battling those who'd tease his foster brother at school. Muhammed had a sense of what was right and wrong and tried to guard Matthew from the world in-between. Most fights they'd lose; slammed against a wall, Muhammed's arms swinging out at the world, Matthew down low, raining in kicks. The kids would snatch Matthew, press him to the ground and pour sand across his nose and mouth, chanting 'Onward Christian Soldier'. Matthew'd look forlorn and helpless at Muhammed and stir such holy anger in him, he'd burst through those holding him back and attack: a wild animal scratching this way, that, to collapse on the ground by Matthew. They'd hold each other there, bruised, covered in dust, sand in their hair. Something impossible was forged there, down on the ground: an absolute trust that whatever else life could thrust at them, they'd face it together. This was unspoken between the boys, this complete, fight formed, dust-ridden-trust.

They'd spend hours together, purposely get lost in fields and not speak a single word. They loved the silence that was choked by others: Halima's brothers who said this was wrong, teachers at school, pastors and imams. They'd splash about naked in the lukewarm streams, or tag team through Super Mario video games. One afternoon in mango season, the sun splashing through the canopy of leaves, they sat under a mango tree and ate every fruit that fell. They got very sick, Halima couldn't explain it and the boys refused to tell. It hurt more than most fights they'd lost but getting beaten was never any fun and after Santana and the Black T-shirt stall, Muhammed thought he could end it all: **– Simple Matthew, if they like us, they won't fight us, and they'll pay us at the same time! You make shirts, I'll talk to them –** Matthew found a sewing machine, an old Singer one tossed in a skip, and taught himself the ins and outs of it. When the treadle broke, he used a drain grate, when the treadle belt broke, he used his own belt, stitching letters cut out of felt; lyrics of songs or playground rhymes, especially rude ones. It worked. Enemies would pause mid-fight, fold up their arms and ask sheepishly **– erm…where'd you get that –** and orders came thick and fast.

A nightclub. Eight years after that, the boys have blossomed to beautiful black men. Matthew is quiet, a typical artist, T-shirt designer, all pencils and pens; Muhammed is charismatic, the salesman. Print by print, stitch by stitch, nightclubs, markets, hawking their tees – free ones to kids and celebrities. A rapper wore one on the cover of an album and that was it, money, rolling in. Limited edition runs of all prints, once they sold out, never again. Their fastest selling shirt was a simple one; Matthew had drawn a white lake such that the black of the shirt seemed like oil spilling into waves. On the back of the shirt he'd written 'Dear Shell, Water No Get Enemy' – lyrics from the Fela Kuti song that everyone loved, its gentle rhythms like waves to ear. Beneath the writing he'd left a space so who bought the shirt could sign their name and they'd wear these T-shirt letters to protests and campaigns against the hell Shell caused. But, they played wild with those shirts, some held together by wooden pins, some strung to wear just once, some of long thin detachable sleeves, some stitched entirely of leaves **– Ayah, remember those crazy things? –** Matthew wants to ask her, still frozen in the gloom, he imagines a smile might ghost Ayah's lips... He doesn't speak. Fingertips grip the white box, shoulders droop deep, feet shuffle on the carpet. He recalls when they sold their ten thousandth shirt.

A nightclub. They celebrate: huge party! Half of Jos city come their way, the journalists, stylists, competitors, all cramped in the bowel of the nightclub, floors slippery wet with hot sweat and Guinness, strobe lights flickering the rhythmic and sizzling stretch of hot flesh, all who got to witness that night said that they were kings!

Halfway through, Muhammed disappears. Matthew asks his girlfriend Zuki **– Where's my bro? –** And follows her jerking thumb down to the bathroom. Muhammed is by the sink, kissing a man.

The door bursts open, a journalist behind screams when he sees this **– Matthew grab him! –** Matt nabs him by his collar, slams the door shut **– Abomination! You'll make my career, when my editors hear you are a fucker of men, you'll be lynched! –** Muhammed's friend bolts out the door. Bass thumps the weak floorboards. Dust falls off the cheap peeling plaster. Matthew, Muhammed and the journalist stand still. Death fills the room. Muhammed offers the journalist cash, who throws his head back, laughing, cackling **– No amount of money will save your life –** Muhammed leans forward, strikes him to the ground. Matthew's eyes narrow in the dirty mirror. The journalist's cries shatter his nerves. The sick sound of fists pounding flesh. Matthew and Muhammed climb out the window as the journalist rises off the floor. Outside, they collapse against the cold walls.

– Matthew – Muhammed speaks **– It's over, I'm done, you know what happens to people like… This is Naija. There's no place to hide. They'll kill me, burn our house down… I have to run. Now, look after mum and // I'm coming –** Matthew says, his voice sudden, brave as blood **– Different city, different country, different world, new shop. // But we've built so much, you can stay here and // No, you can't go on your own, it'll be good for us and the business Muhammed, listen… Listen! We'll be fine. Let me handle this one, we get orders from Cairo, I know someone, let's go eh? That city sucks up Africans like Zuki sucks dick –** Matthew says, inappropriate, warmth in his voice. Muhammed melts with Matthew's kindness. Doesn't trust his voice, just hugs his foster brother, thankful that the cover of darkness hides his tears: two slim streams in the shadow of the club – **Few hours** – Matthew says **– then we disappear.**

Sound –

Flight.

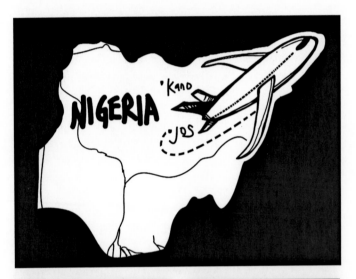

Sheikh Farhat is 56 and thinks he has seen everything. He
presents a stern countenance and hides his good humour
and weak chin beneath a thick beard that most people see
through. He is too quick to smile and the Egyptian sun
twinkles his eyes too much. He has lost one son, so, he is
partial to lost boys wandering the cobbled-stone alleys and
old architecture of Khan el-Khalili, Cairo's biggest market.
He is a carpet seller here and loves the flow of money, the
back and forth of haggling, the smell of all currencies, says
his finger holds the pulse of the world; he loves what he
does with an unmatched passion; he is in charge of two
streets, this one and the next. He knows them intimately,
Warsan's stall of rare spices, the young men who play
backgammon all day. The conmen with tacky souvenirs
for the British, how slips of the Khamsin, the desert wind,
twirls thin scarves Masuma sells and Mahmoud, further
back who snoozes all day jumps when sand grains twang
his instruments **– Voice of an angel –** Farhat murmurs
– You should hear his call to prayer – Farhat sits cross-
legged among his carpets to watch his world walk by.

– MMM – he nods, a cousin passes by **– MMM!! –** he smiles
at a young lady **– MMM? –** he frowns at two black men,
boys to his eyes. Faces unwashed, haven't slept for nights.
The sheikh can tell by how the young one clutching a
white box to his chest, sways, almost falls with each step.
He stares as they walk up to him and the older one speaks
– Sheikh Farhat? they say you are a kind man? –

– MMM They lied! – Farhat replies **– D'you have place
we can stay? We will bring good business. // What
Kinda? –** Farhat asks **– T-shirts –** He adds as the sheikh
begins to laugh **– but a different kind eh? Just give
us a chance. // You have something I can see? –** The
younger one lifts a black shirt from the box into Farhat's
hands. There's an old leaf spread out like a palm print
on its chest. It's held in place by thin black thread. Farhat
holds the T-shirt close to his chest. A gust of the Khamsin
thrusts through his stall and the dried leaf disintegrates to

dust. **– You have name for this? –** Farhat asks **– Yes –** says Matthew **– It's called A Week's Work –** The sheikh, he excuses himself, says something's in his eye, a speck of leaf, and retreats into his stall. **– A Week's Work? –** asks the older one, the young one shrugs, **– No! It's good, name them all –** Farhat returns and the older one speaks **– We have others, better ones –** Farhat studies their faces intently **– OK –** he says **– rest tonight, wash. Tomorrow, new week, you start work. Name? // I'm Matthew, this is Muhammed –** Later that night, Matthew tries Halima, tapping her number into a payphone, but each time he gets an engaged tone.

Two months pass. Business starts slow. 'Matt & Mo' as the boys are now known by street kids who clatter past the patterned stone walls, 'Matt & Mo' know Cairo like it gave them backbones. Sales are slow, but Farhat is confident, he invested money, most of it his own **– S'OK, Nigeria wasn't built in a day –** Muhammed laughs into his cup of mint tea, spilling some on Matthew **– Sss! Muhammed watch it now // Sorry, how's it going eh? // Well, I have an idea –** he says, beckoning Muhammed near. Farhat laughs too and conjures back the night the boys told a treacherous flight to Sudan, a smuggler who got them quickly into Egypt, four days walking the desert terrain and **– here we are –** Muhammed finished. **– But why did you leave? –** Muhammed had a sudden coughing fit and stood out in the cold, Matthew at his side. Returning, they asked if they could rest. Farhat bowed low **– Allah and the Khamsin know best –** he said **– tomorrow! –** He chose a compact stall stacked with white boxes packed with black shirts. Matthew set to work sketching out ideas, Muhammed made friends in Khan el-Khalili **– Business is slow, first thing, get noticed –** Muhammed advised **– I've just the thing –** said Matthew, mischief in his eyes.

Now, the street kids of el-Khalili are fast, I mean The-Khamsin-fast, have almost a 6th sense whereabouts a person's wallet, purse or camera hides; can estimate exactly how much distraction is needed to snatch, leaving tourists surprised at their speed. Their natural enemies: police, dark sunglasses, truncheons at their side.

Bakari was the slowest of the fastest street kids, caught at least once every single week. It's Thursday, the heat is high. Bakari partners with a fake whirling dervish, a guy who copies the Sufi spinning dance. A Sudanese woman drops her bag to clap, and when the shout goes up, Bakari is out fast, scattering past stalls of dried seeds, running low. An officer, hot on his heels closes in, inches from Bakari's shirt. He stretches further, grabs a fistful, yanks, and the back of Bakari's black shirt is in his hand; Bakari rapidly fading in the distance. The market erupts in laughter. He tries to feign anger, but leans against the wall, hugging his sides **– Who did this? Where this come from? –** they point out the black shirt stall **– You did this? –** Matthew nods **– Good work, good work, what you call it? // The... Back-a-rip? // His name! Bakari! Clever, good! So. You make shirt for anyone? // Yes –** Matthew replies **– You make for...us? // Yes –** Matthew smiles, spreads his hands along the counter **– Tell me about yourself –** Over his shoulder Muhammed twirls the fake whirling dervish. They turn down a side street, quiet as mice. Matthew hadn't broached his sexuality, hoped Muhammed would when he felt comfortable. This went unspoken between the boys. Matthew stares after them, squints into the gloom **– Matthew? –** Farhat calls **– You have customer // Matthew –** Ayah calls **– Listen to mother. Matthew? Matthew! Mum is talking to you –**

Matthew shakes off the memory, blinks, breathes and slowly returns to Nigeria. The living room's gloom is thick as guilt, it weighs on his shoulders, it suffocates him **– You left so quickly –** Halima says **– Business opportunity. Good one. Cairo –** Matthew speaks finally **– That not all is it Matthew? –** Ayah says **– You should have told us. We were worried, we didn't hear for months! Years! You return. Muhammed's in a box...this is all you are going to say? //** Matthew stays silent, he licks his lips, thirsty, but won't ask for water **– So, are you happy? –**

asks Halima from the dark **– Was it worth it? –** Matthew, shakes his head from side to side, lifts his face up, sucks back tears. The room swims, he shuts his eyes and tries to conjure Muhammed's face, he thinks of one eve in Cairo, waiting for Muhammed to arrive.

– Matthew? – Farhat asks **– Business going well? What is wrong? // Ahh, it's not enough! –** Matthew speaks into the coming dusk that strides across the sky, crouches on the buildings, a thousand lights in el-Khalilli glow. They don't live here anymore. Matthew misses it. 18 months since they first arrived and the Black T-shirt business is alive! Their shirts are sought after by high-street shops whose staff come all the way here to the Khan. Muhammed's hired staff to meet their demands. They own six stalls now scattered through the market and Matthew's light touch humbles everyone: limited edition calligraphic writings of Qur'ānic verses or Rumi's poems. Anti-government icons, edges sharp as blades, yet supple as water. For the brave ones, bold statements in English and in Arabic: flower-like inscriptions that seem aflame; they blaze in the eyes of the Cairo youth. Their clientele go from the street kids to rich offspring of Egypt's elite who ask 'Matt & Mo' to parties thrown for what reasons they conjure, their job is to come with T-shirts stitched for the night's wild soul. Typically, those nights, Matthew doesn't go, prefers to stay alone in the Zamalek district, in the low-lit apartment they'd come to call home. Now and then Matthew calls Halima, but the line had gone from engaged to dead. He'd stay hunched over, white sheets about him, sketching ideas quick as they come; his shelves are lined with art books, couple on sculpture, in height order they stand up tall, like an installation he curates these walls, flicks through them daily, learns from them all.

He gets up and walks to Muhammed's room. In contrast,
it looks like the Khamsin hit it. T-shirts strewn, this way,
that. Towels dangle from hangers half-damp, half-dragged
across the carpet through plates of food. Matthew laughs
to himself. On Muhammed's shelf: photographs of his
new Egyptian friends. Matthew sits on the bed and flicks
through. There's one photograph of Halima, Muhammed
and Ayah **– I'm not in it, so I must have snapped –**
Matthew thinks and remembers the day after that. They
had learnt about genetics at school, in the kitchen where
Halima stood, Matthew asked nervously **– Where're my
parents? –** Halima, transformed to a thing of stillness,
turned, walked to him and sat down **– Matthew I knew
this day would come. Your parents moved from the
village you were born and the children's home lost
track of them. They loved you, but couldn't feed you,
couldn't afford to send you to school, so I thought**

I could help. I've done alright eh? – Matthew didn't answer. He walked to Halima, hugged her tightly and left the room. The next day he went round to the village and gave every penny he'd saved from the shirts. The villagers, they thanked him endlessly. Mothers clutched their young and hugged him, fathers shook his hand and Matthew felt something he'd never felt before and every month after returned when he could to give as much as he could. In Cairo, a dark shirt falls on the lamp tainting the light that filters through. Matthew sits on the edge of the mattress, lost in his thoughts, bathed in blue. Muhammed staggers in laughing from the party, Matthew stands up – **Bro, it's not enough. // Eh?** – Muhammed says sobering up – **It's not enough, we need to expand and make more money! You should talk to that man you know // Aha? What are we doing with all the cash? We make more than we spend and you give yours to those crazy kids anyway. Why do you do that Matthew? They steal more in a week than we make in a month! We can manage this size, let's not get too big O! // But businesses grow, otherwise they get stagnant, Muhammed you know this, just go and ask him. Do this small thing for me, I left Naija for you // For me?… OK, I'll ask him** –

Matthew waits as the dusk strides low and a thousand lights in el-Khalili glow – **Farhat, he went hours ago, where can he be? // Matthew, Muhammed tries to protect you, there isn't a dishonest drop in his blood. If he says he will come, he will come. Ah, here he is!** – Muhammed embraces Sheikh Farhat, asking of his family. Matthew interrupts – **How did it go? // Are you sure Matthew, this is what you want? OK, I spoke to him, it is done** –

He had spoken with Hassan Winter in Cairo, a French-speaking / PR / publicist / stylist / maestro with a Moroccan-Clark-Kent-in-a-tux thing going for him, thick-frame glasses, he blinked slowly when he talked. He liked women, Muhammed discovered when they talked about European markets **– Matthew –** Hassan said **– I'll make you a star –** arms around them both, his breath of pine trees and toothpaste. He planned everything; trips to six trade shows: 'Fashion' in Helsinki, 'CIEN X CIEN' in Madrid, 'Zoom' in Paris, 'Bread & Butter' in Berlin, tiny one in Florence and a big one in London. Every single shirt would come from Cairo, Matthew hired kids off el-Khalili streets and trained them to copy the simplest designs. Farhat, now quality manager, set to work designing production lines. A hive of activity buzzed in Cairo, Matthew at its centre, Muhammed at his side. At trade shows, a few of the street kids would act out Bakari's back-a-rip trick and when screaming stopped and security arrived, they'd point out the Black T-shirt stall. It worked, everyone flocked to the boys. Buyers, romanced by the roughness of it all, bought Matthew's designs to sell at stores in Amsterdam, Lisbon, Düsseldorf, Minsk, Brussels, Athens, London and more, Farhat called to complain how demand was too great for the boys to match, he laughed as he spoke and Matthew replied **– It's all in a week's work.**

A month later, the boys are back in Cairo, sitting in a café, sipping mint tea and Farhat walks in, a newspaper in his hands **– What is this? –** a frown scars his face. The headline reads of mass graves in Jos, a new one discovered, four hundred killed and goes on to detail the history of the conflict. Farhat sits, confused and shocked **– But You 'Matthew', You 'Muhammed' Go back! Show them friendship work, they kill their brothers! // It's not easy, we –** Matthew stops **– Farhat –** says Muhammed **– we can't return but please don't ask us why –** Farhat leaves not angry but hurt, for he'd come to think of the boys as sons. That night, Muhammed tries Ayah's workplace. The phone call had been a long time coming. Matthew suggested it months ago, but Muhammed, fearing what she might think, begged Matthew **– bro, few more weeks. I'm just not…I dunno…let me think –** A choir of questions choked their throats. What happened to the journalist? When news broke, how had Ayah and Halima coped? Were they questioned by police? Arrested? Lashed? At work, was Halima ever attacked? Was the house burned down? Were they beaten? Were they stoned? Muhammed holds the handset close as Matthew dials the number. They sit, silence about them stiff and coiled in quiet, listening for the tone, the earpiece cupped between both palms **– The number you are calling is out of order, please try again later –** Muhammed heaves a sigh of relief, instantly followed by fear that grows within the hour, hardens every day. They try every week, nothing ever changes, same message every second, every time they call and after six months the boys give up and seek new ways to reach them.

A whole year had passed since the trade fairs; Hassan
suggests a move to London for the client base there grows
bigger by the week. Farhat, thinks this a fine idea and
makes for them a parting gift of a carpet, hand stitched
with early designs, the first ones from the months they'd
arrived penniless in Cairo, years ago. Matthew, humbled
to silence by this, thanks Farhat penitently, who says **– We
still work together eh? This, so whichever new land
you go, you have safe place to stand –** Muhammed
throws the biggest of parties and for once Matthew sparkles
amongst the gathered, the club pumps Arabic hip hop and
the boys are down on the dance floor, spinning… Morning
comes and Farhat prays that Allah and the Khamsin grant
them safe ways to future endeavours in London.

Sound //

Clinking glasses, party, flight airplane to suggest the growth of a business, success.

If you had asked the boys of their first impressions,
Matthew would have talked of the pace of London, how
swift it seemed business happened. Hassan threw them
to the swirling madness of gossip columns, model parties,
the high-street bloggers all made noise that the Black
T-shirt Specialist boys had come. Matthew was shocked to
discover kids who'd collected all their shirts…and it seems
cool to be African in London, Matthew asked Hassan who
shrugged and replied **– Something to do with liberal
guilt and colonial madness; enjoy it! –** If you asked
Muhammed his first thoughts, he'd have talked of a night
in Soho, the first time he saw two men hug, pull back, kiss
each other's eyes, before their lips touched, clutched so
tightly as if all the world had paused for them. Muhammed
dived into this world as if he had an uncultured tongue and
London held the tastes of the planet, he dated like men
were going out of fashion. Though they could afford to rent
two flats, they chose to share one east of the city and when
Muhammed's partners came to visit, Matthew'd suddenly
have work to do, retreat to his bedroom, headphones on.
Muhammed noticed but never said a word. The first shirt
designed in London came from something Muhammed
said of a man he'd met in a club **– It's called G-A-Y, met
one famous sculptor there, Joseph Plié, two months
ago he woke up blind. His birthday is soon, let's do
something nice –** Matthew disappeared into his room,
next morning stepped out with a slogan-ed shirt of black
rubber dots, written in braille: 'We do it best in darkness'
it said. Joseph Plié loved it and when news spread, when
Josep Plié's followers heard, they ordered five thousand
shirts in two days, catapulting Matthew to further fame,
Hassan asking from him new shirts, Muhammed saying **–
slow down Matthew, there's no rush –**

A bar in Mayfair, one year later. Matthew and Hassan
work so tightly, there isn't much for Muhammed to
do. Journalists, wanting the quiet artist focus mostly on

Matthew. Muhammed is never asked about shirts. Instead, with deep concern, they'd lean forward and ask **– What's it like to be a gay Muslim –** Muhammed storms out of these interviews, stops attending photo shoots, with nothing left for him to do, he travels by himself **– New frontiers –** he offers if anyone asks and not many do. In trying to find cheaper material, he discovered the darker sides of this business. He has stories of cotton farming in Mali, Australia, Honduras, Uzbekistan, of factory workers; modern day slaves. He'd just returned from South Africa, talking loudly of shirts **– there is an NGO there eh, they gather homeless boys to cut second-hand shirts to pieces, mix the pieces to make new shirts! Then ship them to New York, Toronto, Milan who sell them at astonishing prices! They even sell to Lagos Matthew! They were cutting up our shirts! We have to start a shop back home, I know we can't return, but –** right then a stranger thrusts his arm into Muhammed's sentence, lets it dangle in the air. Their jaws drop, flabbergasted at the man before them. Muhammed, he doubles over laughing hard, gasping for air, Matthew is breathless. Hassan asks **– Who this? You know this man? // Zebra Santana! You bastard man! What are you doing here?! –**

There is a bubble that surrounds old friends. Its sphere is shaded a beige-blue, inside the atmosphere is ticked with in-jokes, old stories, and a guttural kind of laughter that bellies from the deep. A good-natured kind of chaos leaks from where they sit and infects those around them. An older businessman can't help but smile, the manager offers drinks on the house and two ladies listen in to their talk of running under Nigerian heat, torrential rain and childhood play, they bring Hassan up to speed on exactly who Santana is. Santana marvels that his kick to Matthew's chest, started all this, he demands five per cent of their profits, Muhammed traps him in a headlock, grinding knuckles into his skull. The conversation turns serious. Matthew asks **– How are the killings in Jos? –** And Santana's chin drops **– It's getting worse you know. BBC and FOX call it sectarian violence. It is, but it's** deeper than that. It's political, the presidents holiday in Arab countries and the southern Christians don't trust them. Those Christians who studied in Western schools, run businesses in the Muslim north and when Muslim youth leave Islamic schools, they cannot do the jobs. So, the Christians get rich, Muslims, poor. That's why they want Sharia law, to close Western schools, to claim back business and take back their land. It's economic, it is historic, even climate change plays a part; drought messed up all the land, cattle herders can't feed cows. In Jos it becomes tribal because the Berom people own the land, the Fulani people own the cattle. Beroms are Christians, Fulani, Muslims, so they attack houses of worship where they pray for peace, and blood flows throughout our streets. Thousands massacred, more displaced. Thing is, Naija is the America of West Africa, the land of the best and worst; we are influenced by all sorts. When that Danish cartoonist drew Prophet Muhammed, peace be upon him, there were riots, 15 people killed, is that our business? Eh? And that bastard tried to blow up a plane in the States? What kind of madness is that? – Santana looks to the floor visibly frustrated then stares up at Matthew. Muhammed asks the question and Santana confirms their fears – Yes, they burned your house, Halima and Ayah tried to run but they were caught and lashed in public because they didn't know where you were. It wasn't that severe, still, for a thing natural as…you, one lash is a lash too far. Don't look so surprised Muhammed, I don't care if you are gay, I knew before anyway, whenever we tried to toast girls, your mind was never there! – Quiet falls among them now, the bubble of old friends bursts into sharp shards of worry. Matthew was broken by all this, shaken by the news and hearing that Santana knew before him of Muhammed, his face twists to such deeper fury, Santana says – Sorry, I didn't mean to spoil the mood. They're probably alright, I'll check on them for you? I'm going back home, I don't have a job here so… Wait! Wait! I can start your shop!

And this is how Santana joins the Black T-shirt club. He is hopeless; Masters at Oxford, novice at fashion with his trousers too short, his white gym socks and green suede shoes, his shirt tucked in boxers and he thinks it's cool – **Nah –** Matthew says – **this is how we do –** and proceeds to teach him the rudiments of cool: 1) A pair of Converse All Stars and you are good. 2) No tight shirts, always hide your nipples. 3) Try hard to make it look easy. 4) Whatever happens, say no to pink. 5) Sag your trousers, even wearing suits. But all this just leaves Santana confused.

They spend two weeks planning everything: Matthew chooses new designs, Hassan works out the shipping lines, but when it comes to marketing, how to make a splash, Muhammed like a maestro steps into the light, dazzles with his knowledge of exactly what to do: which rapper to speak to, which school is the trendsetter, which magazine, newspaper, newsletter to hit, send samples to that editor, free shirts to which actor big in Nollywood who is making hit after hit, DJs tumble from his tongue tip and Matthew realises Muhammed loved it; the business in Nigeria, he'd controlled it. At the airport, Santana is presented with a gift for Halima and Ayah. He thinks of this carpet, this hand-stitched rug from Cairo…

The very same one Matthew stands on, now, in the living room south of Jos, in Halima's new house, stuck to this spot, the answers to their questions stuffed in the vast gulf between them and him. He scuffs the patterns slightly, shivering, the white box clutched to his chest, uncomfortable under their spotlight stares. He can't remember when last he slept. He has nightmares, loud ones, dark as earth. There are screams, the weight of things pressing down, footsteps, running, metal snapping skin. Even with eyes closed against the patterns, they blaze bright as knives flashing into him; the fractured torment of what came to pass…

Sometimes, there's order to these thoughts. It comes if Matthew thinks with guilt; thinks back to London, imagines the balcony, Muhammed angry. Muhammed

drains the bottle of Champagne and burps into the night. It is cold. He holds the bottle between his thumb and forefinger, dangles it over the balcony's edge. London teems below; its dance of moving cars and human traffic, like a loose constellation to him. This high up, it is cold. The bottle slips between his thin fingers, families, couples, cops pass below, oblivious to the danger he poses above. Muhammed's caught in the slow-motion fragility of it all, so, when Matthew calls his name, he startles, the bottle slips between his thin grip, he tightens just in time. He ties closed his bathrobe, steps into the room.

Matthew bows low, rising with a flourish, dressed in a grey pin-stripe suit, cufflinks clink against his glass of Scottish scotch and Ribena **– Bro, I'm having your favourite, drink. What'd you think of my bow tie? They're cool you know, you should watch *Doctor Who* like I've been telling you to. Aha? Why aren't you dressed? You're not coming? This is our farewell party Muhammed, are you still angry about…listen, grow up, 'cause I don't have time for // You made the choice without me –** Muhammed speaks in a steel-tipped voice. Matthew clenches his fist, veins stand out, a thick one throbs his forehead **– You weren't around, galavanting across the planet, I made a judgment call, I thought you'd be happy! I won't apologise, it was the right thing to do // You made the choice without me –** Matthew looks to the ground now, his fists limp, the ice cubes wilting in his drink. They had agreed **– till Santana calls, let's not take on any new jobs –** Muhammed travelled to some conference on cotton, Hassan visited, his eyes wide **– Money in China: silk factory, new kind of fabric, one off**

shirt // Where? – Matthew asked **– Guangdong Province, a factory is worked by villagers there –** and Matthew signed the dotted line.

Matthew feels guilt as they pack for China for indefinite a length of time, Hassan waves to them goodbye, Muhammed, a black rock of silence.

Sound //

Flight airplane.

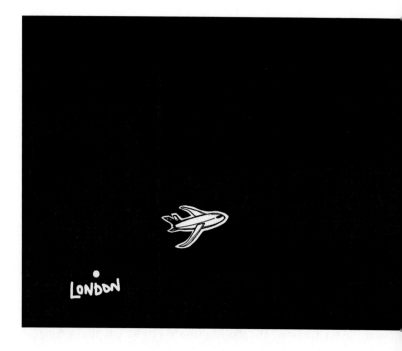

Luo Honshen is 35 and believes in a previous life he'd
made a fine professor. He spent three years in London;
discovered theatre and fashion there before he'd come
home to Zhongshan city. His suits fit well. He strides
with a clipped confidence that hides his lofty thoughts on
Shakespeare and Confucius. He tries to reconcile them as
if lost brothers but Shakespeare is from the gut, Confucius
the head and some things are lost in translation, but his
wife nods, pretends she understands. She loves him, loves
all his achievements including the factory where he works.
Honshen hates the factory he manages but understands
there must be work. For the villagers, it's all they've got
and they know things could be worse. There's a shortage of
jobs, an abundance of people. Don't like the work? Leave,
simple, Honshen thinks as he drives home to his wife and
to his beautiful kids. He stops at the market to buy food he
distributes on Fridays at the factory and buys for his clients,
a box of Guinness, he heard Nigerians liked the drink.

Matthew feels guilt as Muhammed's anger persists
throughout the first week in the City. Avoiding the coldness
of Muhammed's quiet, which deepens or seems to when
he goes near, Matthew hangs out with Luo Honshen,
returns most evenings, late, drunk. Muhammed, furious at
his foster brother, sits by a window, a thick book beside,
awaiting the sun's tireless rise; the cycle to go on. One
evening Matthew comes from a meeting and Mohammed
isn't at home. Not a note in the front room, or a post-it
on the fridge. Matthew worries as darkness swamps the
sky **– Where could he be? He knows no one in China!**
– He paces the living room, drags his feet drinking coffee
after pot after mug of mint tea, his guilt chokes him, his
thoughts run wild **– Is he lying in a gutter? Did they rob**
him? ah! – At 3 a.m. Matthew is overcome with worry,
Mohammed strides in to his **– Where have you been?!**
This is not Cairo, London or even Jos, you can't just…
you didn't even leave a note, tomorrow we're going
to buy mobile phones Muhammed, just look at the

time! – Muhammed laughs, Matthew stops – **I went for a walk OK?** – Matthew nods and Muhammed talks for ten minutes non-stop of all he'd seen. He'd left the city to visit the villages, the broken roads, those who'd tried to rub off his skin, kids who'd asked to touch his hair, their mothers who laughed, starving dogs, the displaced farmers, their reclaimed lands where the government hoped to build new towns. He'd walked out to the vast countryside, where the sky, wide, infinite as ever, humbled his anger at Matthew – **so much money, those kids were hungry // Poverty is poverty, wherever you go** – Matthew says, his voice grey and strained – **Muhammed, sorry I signed the contract without you, it was wrong and // I know** – Muhammed says – **It's OK, just promise it won't happen again.** Muhammed doesn't tell of Wang Bin he'd met in a village, who walked him home, who he'd felt an urgent closeness to, whose smallest brother went up for adoption when their parents couldn't look after them. Wang Bin cried softly as he spoke, his broken English; a noose he struggled through. Mohammed held him close to his chest, Wang Bin lifted up his head, they kissed, hard, on the dirt roads – **I promise** – Matthew says – **it won't happen again** –

Matthew's guilt dims in the weeks after, enough to complete the T-shirt design. Honshen welcomes the work, confides in Matthew something Shakespeare wrote *Neither a borrower nor lender be* and added what Confucius said how the longest journey starts with one step and Matthew was helping with each shirt to feed the workers, free them of debts. Santana rings, he hasn't found Halima – **but don't worry, I'm getting close** – he says. Muhammed spends time with Wang Bin who works at the factory that makes their shirts. Matthew visited the day before but returned, quiet, worried or something… Muhammed decides to see for himself. So this day after, he goes to the factory, stops at the entrance, shocked at the size. The entire shirt is made here, a heaving tangled production line of a thousand workers, crushed, sweating. Muhammed weaves through looking for Wang Bin.

He walks past bags of silkworms cocooned, here the air
must be moist and warm, so windows are shut, doors
closed. The air is thick with germs and dust. Workers strip
down to their waist for the heat, their skin turns sallow
after months of this. If they finish, they go home, but few
meet the task, so sleep on the floor on the boards laid out.
There are children here, least a hundred of them, scruffy,
eyes inflamed, fingers swollen from dipping bare hands
in vats of boiling water; gathering strands of silk from
cocoons, to feed the machines that spin them to thread.
Now, Muhammed trips over pipes of hot water that fill
open vats, part filled with black dye. Inside, its blades slice
the churning water, they slash the black broth like swords
in moonlight. The steam and chemicals rise through the
air. It's poison and workers wear no masks. Muhammed
covers his nose and runs past to the side where the thread
comes out black. The thread is fed to wooden looms and
the women in them weave in the damp, dim light of the
factory, above, one bulb swings **– the fabric is beautiful**
– Muhammed thinks. Wang Bin works where the fabric
is cut. Most crouch, some sit, all waiting their turn. Some
have bandaged hands, some missing fingers, fanning
themselves in the cramped heat. Wang Bin waves excitedly
and breaks Muhammed's heart **– I'm coming –** he says.
He climbs the stairs, crosses the bridge over the open vats,
its blades turning, where Honshen's office and Matthew's
office is. Muhammed wonders where to begin **– he signed
this contract, what should I say to him? –** He leans by
the door, scratches his head and the phone in his pocket
starts to ring **– Hello? Hello? –**

Muhammed, he burst into Matthew's office holding his
phone **– Santana's on the line! He's found them –**
Muhammed turns the speaker phone on **– Hello? –** There
is weight in the air, the stillness before rain **– Hello?
// Muhammed, where are you? // Mama, I'm fine.
// Muhammed, come home, it has been too long
// Mama, things aren't…simple // You are my son
Muhammed, come home –** Muhammed holds his phone,
and there are tears **– OK, I'll leave tomorrow –** Matthew

turns sharply – // err...there's work to do, we'll come in a week or two. // Matthew, I'm going home // We have to finish the job...er...Mama, Santana, we will call you later? // Matthew don't you dare – Matthew shuts the phone – Muhammed, what's up? Why are you in a rush? Business is going well... // Matthew, look around. Why are we here? Have you seen downstairs? those people, how much is Honshen paying them? How much are the shirts? Did we come to China to exploit these people? // No! Muhammed, we are helping them // This is help? // Yes! The factory almost closed, Honshen said, we're putting food on their tables. You said yourself, families are broken, children sent away // Oh, so it's about you eh? Everybody clap for Matthew Zangho, saviour of China. We have our own problems at home. You know how crazy this business is? Desperate cotton pickers sweating for coins, Americans and their slave trade farms, bribing Brazilians to shut up so they sell cheap product across the world. Second-hand shops that 'collect for charity' and sell Matthew, SELL! in Nairobi, Haiti. Chemicals in the fields that cause cancer; those dark-skinned kids in India paid nothing, nothing, and we are one of them! You can map global poverty down to one shirt, one black T-shirt Matthew. From our stall in Jos to this huge factory, something's wrong, something always goes wrong. This is too big for us Matthew, let's go home. We can control things there, we can do this. // Not with you Muhammed, not with you! They'll kill you // I don't care anymore! I'm tired // Why d'you want to go where you can't be... yourself. London, Milan, San Francisco, you can be who you are there! // I don't know who I am. I'm tired, of ticking boxes, I'm gay, I'm an ex-pat, I'm African, I'm a black African, I'm Hausa, I'm Nigerian O! Muslim, this one, that one...journalists asking stupid questions 'What's it like to be... I DON'T KNOW! I just want to be a man again eh? Where people look like us, talk like us, No labels, no colour, no shirts, nothing. They are waiting for us Matthew... Halima, Ayah, our family. We're connecting death here, one shirt at a time.

Let's go home brother // I'M NOT YOUR BROTHER! You ruined my life Muhammed. I wanted to do this in Naija, build this there, but I have it here, now. I'm helping, I'm doing something right. I'm helping them, all those…those men you are fucking! Think I don't know about Wang Bin, that I don't see you?! 15 years we grew up together, sharing the same bed, fighting the same fights, crying together, bleeding and you kept that away from me? ME! Muhammed, ME! You still won't talk to me about it. You faggot! Fuck off! Go back to Naija, I hope they lynch you there, you will burn in hell fire anyway, go and fuck all of them! I don't care!

Muhammed, sorry. I didn't mean that. I just… I'm…

Muhammed is pressed flat against the door, as far from Matthew as he can stand. His hand is to his chest as if stabbed there. He reaches for the door **– Muhammed wait, let's talk –** Muhammed leaves the room, crossing the bridge over the mixing vats, its blades turning, Matthew runs to him **– slow down –** he shouts, he grabs Muhammed's hand, who snatches it back, Matthew holds his shoulder, Muhammed throws his foster brother to the ground, Matthew grabs his feet. Muhammed loses balance.

When it gets here, Muhammed's falling off into the churning vat, its blades turning, that cave his skull in, break through the bone, the black dye mixing with Muhammed's blood, chewing through limbs, twisting him up. There's no order, guilt is not enough. Nothing makes sense and Matthew, he trembles, speechless, in the room. He flinches in Jos, he shudders in the gloom, he quivers on the carpet, Halima watching. From afar, he looks like a child who had lost something old, something deep, a hopelessness grooms his eyes. Closer, by the light that holds him, his still mouth, his hunched shoulders, Matthew looks like a man who had lost everything.

–Tell me how he died – Halima whispers **– WHAT HAPPENED! –** Ayah shouts. Matthew cannot speak. How to begin? What *not* to describe? What might hurt least? **– What's in the box? –** Halima asks **–The first one, the first black shirt // It's true isn't it? You want to close the shop? –** Matthew nods. Ayah stands **– I can't let you, you will not –**

PART 5

Matthew puts the box in the space he'd left and changes into the first black shirt. He runs his thumb along the print and thinks it funny this started it all. There's dust on his hand and he imagines Cairo, the Khamsin blowing through stalls; Farhat prayed for both their souls. He asked no questions over the phone, just did exactly as Matthew told. Hassan argued and finally stopped **– I'll do it Matthew, but this is wrong –** He made phone calls, cancelled every order, gathered unsold shirts from the world and flew them back to this shop in Jos that Matthew stands in now; the shelves stuffed.

One corner holds the silk from China. Matthew cannot look at them for he knows their dye is mixed with Muhammed's blood. Even with eyes closed against the world, every shade of black reminds him of that blood, every black shirt speaks to him of trust, of love, of sex, of money, of God, of Muhammed's father walking home from work. Matthew was devastated when he heard the story but understood what Halima had done. All this comes with the night that hulks, that swims through the curtain, rooting Matthew to the spot. There are thoughts in his emptiness, thunderous ones, soundlessly, he is strangled in his shirt. The tremendous weight of it all.

Matthew lifts the can of gasoline, pours some onto the last box. Lifts the liquid over his head; he tilts till the fluid begins to fall, pours until, drenched to his core, his skin glistens in the dark of his shop. He casts his eyes over the boxes packed with shirts for one last time, takes out a lighter and holds it, waiting, he waits, as the sirens come.

Blackout //

One stage: performer flicking lighter. Once, twice, third time it comes on.

Sound //

Fire, burning.

End.